CHI *8-08*

FRIENDS
OF ACPL

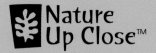
Nature
Up Close™

Sunflowers
Up Close

PowerKiDS
press™
New York

Katie Franks

Published in 2008 by The Rosen Publishing Group, Inc.
29 East 21st Street, New York, NY 10010

First Edition

Editor: Jennifer Way
Book Design: Kate Laczynski

Photo Credits: All illustrations © Studio Stalio.

Library of Congress Cataloging-in-Publication Data

Franks, Katie.
  Sunflowers up close / Katie Franks. — 1st ed.
      p. cm. — (Nature up close)
  Includes index.
  ISBN 978-1-4042-4141-1 (lib. bdg.)
  1. Sunflowers—Juvenile literature. I. Title.
  QK495.C74F73 2008
  583'.99—dc22
                                        2007023198

Manufactured in the United States of America

Contents

Sunflowers 4

The Head 8

A Sunflower's Life 14

Words to Know 24

Index 24

Web Sites.................................24

Sunflowers are tall, yellow flowers. Sunflowers can be more than 10 feet (3 m) tall.

5

This drawing shows the many parts of a sunflower. A few of these are the head, leaves, **stem**, and the **roots**.

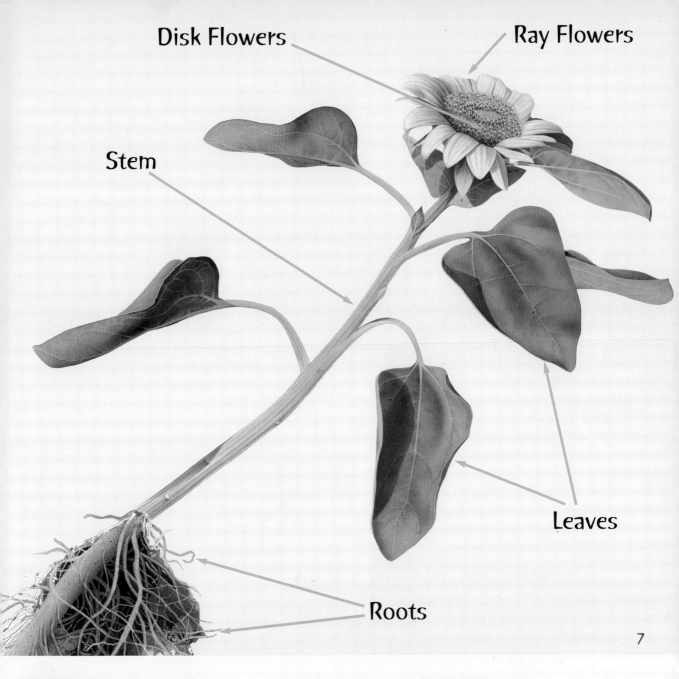

Disk Flowers

Ray Flowers

Stem

Leaves

Roots

The head of the flower is made up of many smaller flowers! These smaller flowers are called ray flowers and disk flowers.

Disk Flowers

Ray Flowers

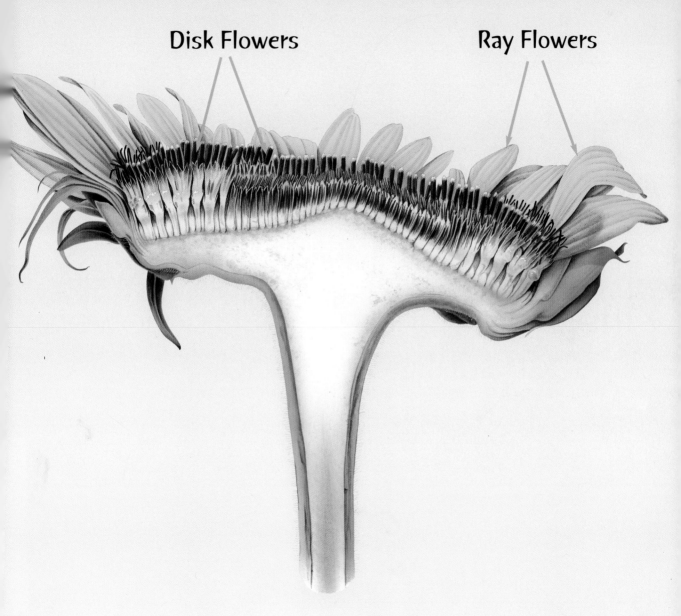

This is a close-up of a disk flower.
There are hundreds of disk flowers
in each sunflower head.

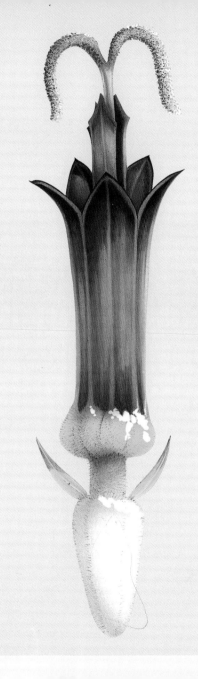

The disk flower is the part of the sunflower that makes seeds. Many birds like to eat sunflower seeds.

13

These drawings show the life steps of a sunflower. Over time, the disk flowers grow and get heavy with seeds and later die.

1

2

3

Bees are important to sunflowers. Bees help move **pollen** between flowers. Pollen is what helps flowers make seeds.

There are bugs that are not good for sunflowers. The sunflower seed weevil lays its eggs in sunflowers.

Native Americans were the first people to grow sunflowers. They grew them in North America's Great Plains.

Today sunflowers are grown in many places around the world, not just the Great Plains. The Great Plains are orange on this map.

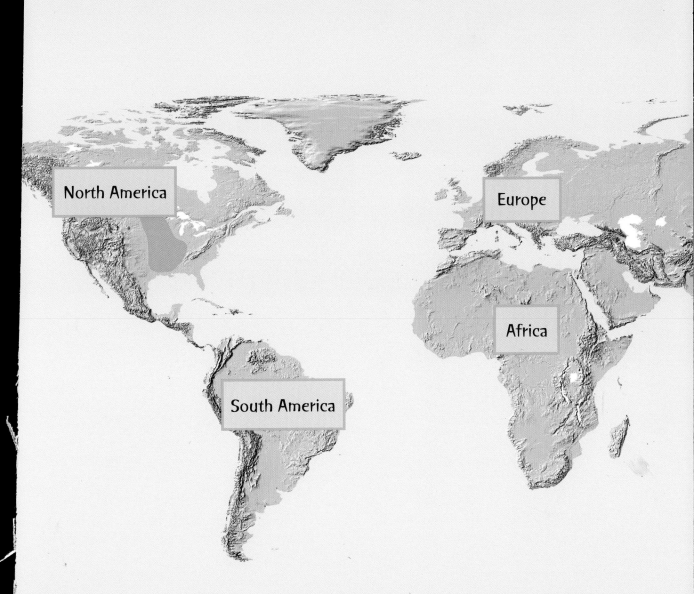

North America

Europe

Africa

South America

23

Words to Know

pollen

roots

stem

Index

G
Great Plains,
   20, 22

H
head, 6, 8, 10

P
part(s), 6, 12

S
seed(s), 12, 14,
   16, 18

W
world, 22

Web Sites

Due to the changing nature of Internet links, PowerKids Press has developed an online list of Web sites related to the subject of this book. This site is updated regularly. Please use this link to access the list: www.powerkidslinks.com/nuc/sflow/